VLADIMIR
NABOKOV

NOW REMEMBER

D0544796

PENGUIN BOOKS

PENGUIN BOOKS

Published by the Penguin Group. Penguin Books Ltd, 27 Wrights Lane, London
w8 5tz, England. Penguin Books USA Inc., 375 Hudson Street, New York,
New York 10014, USA. Penguin Books Australia Ltd, Ringwood, Victoria, Australia.
Penguin Books Canada Ltd, 10 Alcorn Avenue, Toronto, Ontario, Canada m4v 3b2.
Penguin Books (NZ) Ltd, 182 – 190 Wairau Road, Auckland 10, New Zealand · Penguin
Books Ltd, Registered Offices: Harmondsworth, Middlesex, England · These
extracts are from *Speak, Memory* by Vladimir Nabokov, revised and expanded edition
published by Weidenfeld & Nicolson 1967. Published in Penguin Books 1969. This
edition published 1996. Copyright © 1947, 1948, 1949, 1950, 1951 by Vladimir
Nabokov. Copyright © Vladimir Nabokov, 1967. All rights reserved · Typeset by
Rowland Phototypesetting Ltd, Bury St Edmunds, Suffolk. Printed in England by
Clays Ltd, St Ives plc · Except in the United States of America, this book is sold
subject to the condition that it shall not, by way of trade or otherwise, be lent,
re-sold, hired out, or otherwise circulated without the publisher's prior consent in
any form of binding or cover other than that in which it is published and without
a similar condition including this condition being imposed on the subsequent
purchaser · 10 9 8 7 6 5 4 3 2 1

As far back as I remember myself (with interest, with amusement, seldom with admiration or disgust), I have been subject to mild hallucinations. Some are aural, others are optical, and by none have I profited much. The fatidic accents that restrained Socrates or egged on Joaneta Darc have degenerated with me to the level of something one happens to hear between lifting and clapping down the receiver of a busy party-line telephone. Just before falling asleep, I often become aware of a kind of one-sided conversation going on in an adjacent section of my mind, quite independently from the actual trend of my thoughts. It is a neutral, detached, anonymous voice, which I catch saying words of no importance to me whatever – an English or a Russian sentence, not even addressed to me, and so trivial that I hardly dare give samples, lest the flatness I wish to convey be marred by a molehill of sense. This silly phenomenon seems to be the auditory counterpart of certain praedormitary visions, which I also know well. What I mean is not the bright mental image (as, for instance, the face of a beloved parent long dead) conjured up by a wing-stroke of the will; *that* is one of the bravest movements a human spirit can make. Nor am I alluding to the so-called *muscae volitantes* – shadows cast upon the retinal rods by motes in the vitreous humor, which are seen as transparent threads drifting across the visual field. Perhaps nearer to the hypnagogic mirages I am thinking of is the colored spot, the stab of an afterimage, with which the lamp one had just turned off wounds the palpebral night. However, a shock of this sort is not really a necessary starting point for the slow, steady development of the visions that pass before my closed eyes. They come and go, without the drowsy observer's participation, but are essentially different from dream pictures for he is still master of his senses. They are often grotesque. I am pestered by roguish profiles, by some coarse-featured and florid dwarf with a swelling nostril or ear. At times, however, my photisms take on a rather soothing *flou* quality, and then I see – projected, as it were, upon the inside of the eyelid – gray figures walking between beehives, or small black parrots gradually vanishing among mountain snows, or a mauve remoteness melting beyond moving masts.

On top of all this I present a fine case of colored hearing. Perhaps 'hearing' is not quite accurate, since the color sensation seems to be produced by the very act of my orally forming a given letter while I imagine its outline. The long *a* of the English alphabet (and it is this alphabet I have in mind farther on unless otherwise stated) has for me the tint of weathered wood, but a French *a* evokes polished ebony. This black group also includes hard *g* (vulcanized rubber) and *r* (a sooty rag being ripped). Oatmeal *n*, noodle-limp *l*, and the ivory-backed hand mirror of *o* take care of the whites. I am puzzled by my French *on* which I see as the brimming tension-surface of alcohol in a small glass. Passing on to the blue group, there is steely *x*, thundercloud *z*, and huckleberry *k*. Since a subtle interaction exists between sound and shape, I see *q* as browner than *k*, while *s* is not the light blue of *c*, but a curious mixture of azure and mother-of-pearl. Adjacent tints do not merge, and diphthongs do not have special colors of their own, unless represented by a single character in some other language (thus the fluffy-gray, three-stemmed Russian letter that stands for *sh*, a letter as old as the rushes of the Nile, influences its English representation).

I hasten to complete my list before I am interrupted. In the green group, there are alder-leaf *f*, the unripe apple of *p*, and pistachio *t*. Dull green, combined somehow with violet, is the best I can do for *w*. The yellows comprise various *e*'s and *i*'s, creamy *d*, bright-golden *y*, and *u* whose alphabetical value I can express only by 'brassy with an olive sheen.' In the brown group, there are the rich rubbery tone of soft *g*, paler *j*, and the drab shoelace of *h*. Finally, among the reds, *b* has the tone called burnt sienna by painters, *m* is a fold of pink flannel, and today I have at last perfectly matched *v* with 'Rose Quartz' in Maerz and Paul's *Dictionary of Color*. The word for rainbow, a primary, but decidedly muddy, rainbow, is in my private language the hardly pronounceable: *kzspygv*. The first author to discuss *audition colorée* was, as far as I know, an albino physician in 1812, in Erlangen.

The confessions of a synesthete must sound tedious and pretentious to those who are protected from such leakings and drafts by more solid walls than mine are. To my mother, though, this all seemed quite normal. The matter came up, one day in my seventh year, as I was using a heap of old alphabet blocks to build a tower. I casually remarked to her that their colors were all wrong. We discovered then that some of her letters had the same tint as mine and that, besides, she was optically affected by musical notes. These evoked no chromatisms in me whatsoever. Music, I regret to say, affects me merely as an arbitrary succession of more or less irritating

3

sounds. Under certain emotional circumstances I can stand the spasms of a rich violin, but the concert piano and all wind instruments bore me in small doses and flay me in larger ones. Despite the number of operas I was exposed to every winter (I must have attended *Ruslan* and *Pikovaya Dama* at least a dozen times in the course of half as many years), my weak responsiveness to music was completely overrun by the visual torment of not being able to read over Pimen's shoulder or of trying in vain to imagine the hawkmoths in the dim bloom of Juliet's garden.

My mother did everything to encourage the general sensitiveness I had to visual stimulation. How many were the aquarelles she painted for me; what a revelation it was when she showed me the lilac tree that grows out of mixed blue and red! Sometimes, in our St Petersburg house, from a secret compartment in the wall of her dressing room (and my birth room), she would produce a mass of jewelry for my bedtime amusement. I was very small then, and those flashing tiaras and chokers and rings seemed to me hardly inferior in mystery and enchantment to the illumination in the city during imperial fêtes, when, in the padded stillness of a frosty night, giant monograms, crowns, and other armorial designs, made of colored electric bulbs – sapphire, emerald, ruby – glowed with a kind of charmed constraint above snow-lined cornices on housefronts along residential streets.

My numerous childhood illnesses brought my mother and me still closer together. As a little boy, I showed an abnormal aptitude for mathematics, which I completely lost in my singularly talentless youth. This gift played a horrible part in tussles with quinsy or scarlet fever, when I felt enormous spheres and huge numbers swell relentlessly in my aching brain. A foolish tutor had explained logarithms to me much too early, and I had read (in a British publication, the *Boy's Own Paper*, I believe) about a certain Hindu calculator who in exactly two seconds could find the seventeenth root of, say, 3529471145760275132301897342055866171392 (I am not sure I have got this right; anyway the root was 212). Such were the monsters that thrived on my delirium, and the only way to prevent them from crowding me out of myself was to kill them by extracting their hearts. But they were far too strong, and I would sit up and laboriously form garbled sentences as I tried to explain things to my mother. Beneath my delirium, she recognized sensations she had known herself, and her understanding would bring my expanding universe back to a Newtonian norm.

The future specialist in such dull literary lore as autoplagiarism will like to collate a protagonist's experience in my novel *The Gift* with the original event. One day, after a long illness, as I lay in bed still very weak, I found myself basking in an unusual euphoria of lightness and repose. I knew my mother had gone to buy me the daily present that made those convalescences so delightful. What it would be this time I could not guess, but through the crystal of my strangely translucent state

I vividly visualized her driving away down Morskaya Street toward Nevski Avenue. I distinguished the light sleigh drawn by a chestnut courser. I heard his snorting breath, the rhythmic clacking of his scrotum, and the lumps of frozen earth and snow thudding against the front of the sleigh. Before my eyes and before those of my mother loomed the hind part of the coachman, in his heavily padded blue robe, and the leather-encased watch (twenty minutes past two) strapped to the back of his belt, from under which curved the pumpkin-like folds of his huge stuffed rump. I saw my mother's seal furs and, as the icy speed increased, the muff she raised to her face – that graceful, winter-ride gesture of a St Petersburg lady. Two corners of the voluminous spread of bearskin that covered her up to the waist were attached by loops to the two side knobs of the low back of her seat. And behind her, holding on to these knobs, a footman in a cockaded hat stood on his narrow support above the rear extremities of the runners.

Still watching the sleigh, I saw it stop at Treumann's (writing implements, bronze baubles, playing cards). Presently, my mother came out of this shop followed by the footman. He carried her purchase, which looked to me like a pencil. I was astonished that she did not carry so small an object herself, and this disagreeable question of dimensions caused a faint renewal, fortunately very brief, of the 'mind dilation effect' which I hoped had gone with the fever. As she was being tucked up again in the sleigh, I watched the vapor exhaled by all, horse included. I watched, too, the familiar pouting movement she made to distend the network of her close-fitting veil drawn too tight over her face, and as I write this, the touch of reticulated tenderness that my lips used to feel when I kissed her veiled cheek comes back to me – *flies* back to me with a shout of joy out of the snow-blue, blue-windowed (the curtains are not yet drawn) past.

A few minutes later, she entered my room. In her arms she held a big parcel. It had been, in my vision, greatly reduced in size – perhaps, because I subliminally corrected what logic warned me might still be the dreaded remnants of delirium's dilating world. Now the object proved to be a giant polygonal Faber pencil, four feet long and correspondingly thick. It had been hanging as a showpiece in the shop's window, and she presumed I had coveted it, as I coveted all things that were not quite purchasable. The shopman had been obliged to ring up an agent, a 'Doctor' Libner (as if the transaction possessed indeed some pathological import). For an awful moment, I wondered whether the point was made of real graphite. It was. And some years later I satisfied myself, by drilling a hole in the side, that the lead went right through the whole length – a perfect case of art for art's sake on the part of Faber and Dr Libner since the pencil was far too big for use and, indeed, was not meant to be used.

'Oh yes,' she would say as I mentioned this or that unusual sensation. 'Yes, I know all that,' and with a somewhat eerie ingenuousness she would discuss such things as double sight, and little raps in the woodwork of tripod tables, and premonitions, and the feeling of the *déjà vu*. A streak of sectarianism ran through her direct ancestry. She went to church only at Lent and Easter. The schismatic mood revealed itself in her healthy distaste for the ritual of the Greek Catholic Church and for its priests. She found a deep appeal in the moral and poetical side of the Gospels, but felt no need in the support of any dogma. The appalling insecurity of an afterlife and its lack of privacy did not enter her thoughts. Her intense and pure religiousness took the form of her having equal faith in the existence of another world and in the impossibility of comprehending it in terms of earthly life. All one could do was to glimpse, amid the haze and the chimeras, something real ahead, just as persons endowed with an unusual persistence of diurnal cerebration are able to perceive in their deepest sleep, somewhere beyond the throes of an entangled and inept nightmare, the ordered reality of the waking hour.

3

To love with all one's soul and leave the rest to fate, was the simple rule she heeded. '*Vot zapomni* [now remember],' she would say in conspiratorial tones as she drew my attention to this or that loved thing in Vyra – a lark ascending the curds-and-whey sky of a dull spring day, heat lightning taking pictures of a distant line of trees in the night, the palette of maple leaves on brown sand, a small bird's cuneate footprints on new snow. As if feeling that in a few years the tangible part of her world would perish, she cultivated an extraordinary consciousness of the various time marks distributed throughout our country place. She cherished her own past with the same retrospective fervor that I now do her image and my past. Thus, in a way, I inherited an exquisite simulacrum – the beauty of intangible property, unreal estate – and this proved a splendid training for the endurance of later losses. Her special tags and imprints became as dear and as sacred to me as they were to her. There was the room which in the past had been reserved for her mother's pet hobby, a chemical laboratory; there was the linden tree marking the spot, by the side of the road that sloped up toward the village of Gryazno (accented on the ultima), at the steepest bit where one preferred to take one's 'bike by the horns' (*bïka za roga*) as my father, a dedicated cyclist, liked to say, and where he had proposed; and there was, in the so-called 'old' park, the obsolete tennis court, now a region of moss, mole-heaps, and mushrooms, which had been the scene of gay rallies in the eighties and nineties (even her grim father would shed his coat and give the heaviest racket an appraisive shake) but which, by the time I was ten, nature had effaced with the thoroughness of a felt eraser wiping out a geometrical problem.

By then, an excellent modern court had been built at the end of the 'new' part of the park by skilled workmen imported from Poland for that purpose. The wire mesh of an ample enclosure separated it from the flowery meadow that framed its clay. After a damp night the surface acquired a brownish gloss and the white lines would be repainted with liquid chalk from a green pail by Dmitri, the smallest and oldest of our gardeners, a meek, black-booted, red-shirted dwarf slowly retreating, all hunched up, as his paintbrush went down the line. A pea-tree hedge (the 'yellow acacia' of northern Russia), with a midway opening, corresponding to the court's screen door, ran parallel to the enclosure and to a path dubbed *tropinka Sfinksov* ('path of the Sphingids') because of the hawkmoths visiting at dusk the fluffy lilacs along the border that faced the hedge and likewise broke in the middle. This path formed the bar of a great T whose vertical was the alley of slender oaks, 9 my mother's coevals, that traversed (as already said) the new park through its entire length. Looking down that avenue from the base of the T near the drive one could make out quite distinctly the bright little gap five hundred yards away - or fifty years away from where I am now. Our current tutor or my father, when he stayed with us in the country, invariably had my brother for partner in our temperamental family doubles. 'Play!' my mother would cry in the old manner as she put her little foot forward and bent her white-hatted head to ladle out an assiduous but feeble serve. I got easily cross with her, and she, with the ballboys, two barefooted peasant lads (Dmitri's pug-nosed grandson and the twin brother of pretty Polenka, the head coachman's daughter). The northern summer became tropical around harvest time. Scarlet Sergey would stick his racket between his knees and laboriously wipe his glasses. I see my butterfly net propped against the enclosure – just in case. Wallis Myers' book on lawn tennis lies open on a bench, and after every exchange my father (a first-rate player, with a cannonball service of the Frank Riseley type and a beautiful 'lifting drive') pedantically inquires of my brother and me whether the 'follow-through,' that state of grace, has descended upon us. And sometimes a prodigious cloudburst would cause us to huddle under a shelter at the corner of the court while old Dmitri would be sent to fetch umbrellas and raincoats from the house. A quarter of an hour later he would reappear under a mountain of clothing in the vista of the long avenue which as he advanced would regain its leopard spots with the sun blazing anew and his huge burden unneeded.

She loved all games of skill and gambling. Under her expert hands, the thousand bits of a jigsaw puzzle gradually formed an English hunting scene; what had seemed to be the limb of a horse would turn out to belong to an elm and the hitherto unplaceable piece would snugly fill up a gap in the mottled background, affording one the delicate thrill of an abstract and yet tactile satisfaction. At one time, she was very fond of poker, which had reached St Petersburg society via diplomatic circles, so that some of the combinations came with pretty French names – *brelan* for 'three of a kind,' *couleur* for 'flush,' and so on. The game in use was the regular 'draw poker,' with, occasionally, the additional tingle of jackpots and an omnivicarious joker. In town, she often played poker at the houses of friends until three in the morning, a society recreation in the last years before World War One; and later, in exile, she used to imagine (with the same wonder and dismay with which she recalled old Dmitri) the chauffeur Pirogov who still seemed to be waiting for her in the relentless frost of an unending night, although, in his case, rum-laced tea in a hospitable kitchen must have gone a long way to assuage those vigils.

One of the greatest pleasures in summer was the very Russian sport of *hodit' po gribï* (looking for mushrooms). Fried in butter and thickened with sour cream, her delicious finds appeared regularly on the dinner table. Not that the gustatory moment mattered much. Her main delight was in the quest, and this quest had its rules. Thus, no agarics were taken; all she picked were species belonging to the edible section of the genus *Boletus* (tawny *edulis*, brown *scaber*, red *aurantiacus*, and a few close allies), called 'tube mushrooms' by some and coldly defined by mycologists as 'terrestrial, fleshy, putrescent, centrally stipitate fungi.' Their compact pilei – tight-fitting in infant plants, robust and appetizingly domed in ripe ones – have a smooth (not lamellate) under-surface and a neat, strong stem. In classical simplicity of form, boletes differ considerably from the 'true mushroom,' with its preposterous gills and effete stipal ring. It is, however, to the latter, to the lowly and ugly agarics, that nations with timorous taste buds limit their knowledge and appetite, so that to the Anglo–American lay mind the aristocratic boletes are, at best, reformed toadstools.

Rainy weather would bring out these beautiful plants in profusion under the firs, birches and aspens in our park, especially in its older part, east of the carriage road that divided the park in two. Its shady recesses would then harbor that special boletic reek which makes a Russian's nostrils dilate – a dark, dank, satisfying blend of damp moss, rich earth, rotting leaves. But one had to poke and peer for a goodish while among the wet underwood before something really nice, such as a family of bonneted baby *edulis* or the marbled variety of *scaber*, could be discovered and carefully teased out of the soil.

On overcast afternoons, all alone in the drizzle, my mother, carrying a basket (stained blue on the inside by somebody's whortleberries), would set out on a long collecting tour. Toward dinnertime, she could be seen emerging from the nebulous depths of a park alley, her small figure cloaked and hooded in greenish-brown wool, on which countless droplets of moisture made a kind of mist all around her. As she came nearer from under the dripping trees and caught sight of me, her face would show an odd, cheerless expression, which might have spelled poor luck, but which I knew was the tense, jealously contained beatitude of the successful hunter. Just before reaching me, with an abrupt, drooping movement of the arm and shoulder and a 'Pouf!' of magnified exhaustion, she would let her basket sag, in order to stress its weight, its fabulous fullness.

Near a white garden bench, on a round garden table of iron, she would lay out her boletes in concentric circles to count and sort them. Old ones, with spongy, dingy flesh, would be eliminated, leaving the young and the crisp. For a moment, before they were bundled away by a servant to a place she knew nothing about, to a doom that did not interest her, she would stand there admiring them, in a glow of quiet contentment. As often happened at the end of a rainy day, the sun might cast a lurid gleam just before setting, and there, on the damp round table, her mushrooms would lie, very colorful, some bearing traces of extraneous vegetation – a grass blade sticking to a viscid fawn cap, or moss still clothing the bulbous base of a dark-stippled stem. And a tiny looper caterpillar would be there, too, measuring, like a child's finger and thumb, the rim of the table, and every now and then stretching upward to grope, in vain, for the shrub from which it had been dislodged.

4

Not only were the kitchen and the servants' hall never visited by my mother, but they stood as far removed from her consciousness as if they were the corresponding quarters in a hotel. My father had no inclination, either, to run the house. But he did order the meals. With a little sigh, he would open a kind of album laid by the butler on the dinner table after dessert and in his elegant, flowing hand write down the menu for the following day. He had a peculiar habit of letting his pencil or fountain pen vibrate just above the paper while he pondered the next ripple of words. My mother nodded a vague consent to his suggestions or made a wry face. Nominally, the housekeeping was in the hands of her former nurse, at that time a bleary, incredibly wrinkled old woman (born a slave around 1830) with the small face of a melancholy tortoise and big shuffling feet. She wore a nunnish brown dress and gave off a slight but unforgettable smell of coffee and decay. Her dreaded congratulation on our birthdays and namedays was the serfage kiss on the shoulder. Age had developed in her a pathological stinginess, especially in regard to sugar and preserves, so that by degrees, and with the sanction of my parents, other domestic arrangements, kept secret from her, had quietly come into force. Without knowing it (the knowledge would have broken her heart), she remained dangling as it were, from her own key ring, while my mother did her best to allay with soothing words the suspicions that now and then flitted across the old woman's weakening mind. Sole mistress of her moldy and remote little kingdom, which she thought was the real one (we would have starved had it been so), she was followed by the mocking glances of lackeys and maids as she steadily plodded through long corridors to store away half an apple or a couple of broken Petit-Beurre biscuits she had found on a plate.

Meanwhile, with a permanent staff of about fifty servants and no questions asked, our city household and country place were the scenes of a fantastic merry-go-round of theft. In this, according to nosy old aunts, whom nobody heeded but who proved to be right after all, the chief cook Nikolay Andreevich and the head gardener Egor, both staid-looking, bespectacled men with the hoary temples of trusty retainers, were the two masterminds. When confronted with stupendous and incomprehensible bills, or a sudden extinction of garden strawberries and hothouse peaches, my father, a jurist and a statesman, felt professionally vexed at not being able to cope with the economics of his own home; but every time a complicated case of larceny came to light, some legal doubt or scruple prevented him from doing anything about it. When common sense required the firing of a rascally servant, the man's little son would as likely as not fall desperately ill, and the resolution to get the best doctors in town for him would cancel all other considerations. So, with one thing and another, my father preferred to leave the whole housekeeping situation in a state of precarious equilibrium (not devoid of a certain quiet humor), with my mother deriving considerable comfort from the hope that her old nurse's illusory world would not be shattered.

My mother knew well how hurtful a broken illusion could be. The most trifling disappointment took on for her the dimensions of a major disaster. One Christmas Eve, in Vyra, not long before her fourth baby was to be born, she happened to be laid up with a slight ailment and made my brother and me (aged, respectively, five and six) promise not to look into the Christmas stockings that we would find hanging from our bedposts on the following morning but to bring them over to her room and investigate them there, so that she could watch and enjoy our pleasure. Upon awakening, I held a furtive conference with my brother, after which, with eager hands, each felt his delightfully crackling stocking, stuffed with small presents; these we cautiously fished out one by one, undid the ribbons, loosened the tissue paper, inspected everything by the weak light that came through a chink in the shutters, wrapped up the little things again, and crammed them back where they had been. I next recall our sitting on our mother's bed, holding those lumpy stockings and doing our best to give the performance she had wanted to see; but we had so messed up the wrappings, so amateurish were our renderings of enthusiastic surprise (I can see my brother casting his eyes upward and exclaiming, in imitation of our new French governess, '*Ah, que c'est beau!*'), that, after observing us for a moment, our audience burst into tears. A decade passed. World War One started. A crowd of patriots and my uncle Ruka stoned the German Embassy. *Peterburg* was sunk to *Petrograd* against all rules of nomenclatorial priority. Beethoven turned out to be Dutch. The newsreels showed photogenic explosions, the spasm of a cannon, Poincaré in his leathern leggings, bleak puddles, the poor little Tsarevich in Circassian uniform with dagger and cartridges, his tall sisters so dowdily dressed, long railway trains crammed with troops. My mother set up a private hospital for wounded soldiers. I remember her, in the fashionable nurse's gray-and-white uniform she abhorred, denouncing with the same childish tears the impenetrable meekness of those crippled peasants and the ineffectiveness of part-time compassion. And, still later, when in exile, reviewing the past, she would often accuse herself (unjustly as I see it now) of having been less affected by the misery of man than by the emotional load man dumps upon innocent nature – old trees, old horses, old dogs.

Her particular fondness for brown dachshunds puzzled my critical aunts. In the family albums illustrating her young years, there was hardly a group that did not include one such animal – usually with some part of its flexible body blurred and always with the strange, paranoiac eyes dachshunds have in snapshots.

A couple of obese old-timers, Box I and Loulou, still lolled in the sunshine on the porch when I was a child. Sometime in 1904 my father bought at a dog show in Munich a pup which grew into the bad-tempered but wonderfully handsome Trainy (as I named him because of his being as long and as brown as a sleeping car). One of the musical themes of my childhood is Trainy's hysterical tongue, on the trail of the hare he never got, in the depths of our Vyra park, whence he would return at dusk (after my anxious mother had stood whistling for a long time in the oak avenue) with the old corpse of a mole in his jaws and burs in his ears. Around 1915, his hind legs became paralyzed, and until he was chloroformed, he would dismally drag himself over long, glossy stretches of parquet floor like a *cul de jatte*. Then somebody gave us another pup, Box II, whose grandparents had been Dr Anton Chekhov's Quina and Brom. This final dachshund followed us into exile, and as late as 1930, in a suburb of Prague (where my widowed mother spent her last years, on a small pension provided by the Czech government), he could be still seen going for reluctant walks with his mistress, waddling far behind in a huff, tremendously old and furious with his long Czech muzzle of wire – an émigré dog in a patched and ill-fitting coat.

During our last two Cambridge years, my brother and I used to spend vacations in Berlin, where our parents with the two girls and ten-year-old Kirill occupied one of those large, gloomy, eminently bourgeois apartments that I have let to so many émigré families in my novels and short stories. On the night of 28 March 1922, around ten o'clock, in the living room where as usual my mother was reclining on the red-plush corner couch, I happened to be reading to her Blok's verse on 17

Italy – had just got to the end of the little poem about Florence, which Blok compares to the delicate, smoky bloom of an iris, and she was saying over her knitting, 'Yes, yes, Florence does look like a *dïmnïy iris*, how true! I remember –' when the telephone rang.

After 1923, when she moved to Prague, and I lived in Germany and France, I was unable to visit her frequently; nor was I with her at her death, which occurred on the eve of World War Two. Whenever I did manage to go to Prague, there was always that initial pang one feels just before time, caught unawares, again dons its familiar mask. In the pitiable lodgings she shared with her dearest companion, Evgeniya Konstantinovna Hofeld (1884–1957), who had replaced, in 1914, Miss Greenwood (who, in her turn, had replaced Miss Lavington) as governess of my two sisters (Olga, born 5 January 1903, and Elena, born 31 March 1906), albums, in which, during the last years, she had copied out her favorite poems, from Maykov to Mayakovski, lay around her on odds and ends of decrepit, secondhand furniture. A cast of my father's hand and a watercolor picture of his grave in the Greek-Catholic cemetery of Tegel, now in East Berlin, shared a shelf with émigré writers' books, so prone to disintegration in their cheap paper covers. A soapbox covered with green cloth supported the dim little photographs in crumbling frames she liked to have near her couch. She did not really need them, for nothing had been lost. As a company of traveling players carry with them everywhere, while they still remember their lines, a windy heath, a misty castle, an enchanted island, so she had with her all that her soul had stored. With great clarity, I can see her sitting at a table and serenely considering the laid-out cards of a game of solitaire: she leans on her left elbow and presses to her cheek the free thumb of her left hand, in which, close to her mouth, she holds a cigarette, while her right hand stretches toward the next card. The double gleam on her fourth finger is two marriage rings – her own and my father's, which, being too large for her, is fastened to hers by a bit of black thread.

Whenever in my dreams I see the dead, they always appear silent, bothered, strangely depressed, quite unlike their dear, bright selves. I am aware of them, without any astonishment, in surroundings they never visited during their earthly existence, in the house of some friend of mine they never knew. They sit apart, frowning at the floor, as if death were a dark taint, a shameful family secret. It is certainly not then – not in dreams – but when one is wide awake, at moments of robust joy and achievement, on the highest terrace of consciousness, that mortality has a chance to peer beyond its own limits, from the mast, from the past and its castle tower. And although nothing much can be seen through the mist, there is somehow the blissful feeling that one is looking in the right direction.

The kind of Russian family to which I belonged – a kind now extinct – had, among other virtues, a traditional leaning toward the comfortable products of Anglo-Saxon civilization. Pears' Soap, tar-black when dry, topaz-like when held to the light between wet fingers, took care of one's morning bath. Pleasant was the decreasing weight of the English collapsible tub when it was made to protrude a rubber underlip and disgorge its frothy contents into the slop pail. 'We could not improve the cream, so we improved the tube,' said the English toothpaste. At breakfast, Golden Syrup imported from London would entwist with its glowing coils the revolving spoon from which enough of it had slithered onto a piece of Russian bread and butter. All sorts of snug, mellow things came in a steady procession from the English Shop on Nevski Avenue: fruitcakes, smelling salts, playing cards, picture puzzles, striped blazers, talcum-white tennis balls.

I learned to read English before I could read Russian. My first English friends were four simple souls in my grammar – Ben, Dan, Sam and Ned. There used to be a great deal of fuss about their identities and whereabouts – 'Who is Ben?' 'He is Dan.' 'Sam is in bed,' and so on. Although it all remained rather stiff and patchy (the compiler was handicapped by having to employ – for the initial lessons, at least – words of not more than three letters), my imagination somehow managed to obtain the necessary data. Wan-faced, big-limbed, silent nitwits, proud in the possession of certain tools ('Ben has an axe'), they now drift with a slow-motioned slouch across the remotest backdrop of memory; and, akin to the mad alphabet of an optician's chart, the grammar-book lettering looms again before me.

The schoolroom was drenched with sunlight. In a sweating glass jar, several spiny caterpillars were feeding on nettle leaves (and ejecting interesting, barrel-shaped pellets of olive-green frass). The oilcloth that covered the round table smelled of glue. Miss Clayton smelled of Miss Clayton. Fantastically, gloriously, the blood-colored alcohol of the outside thermometer had risen to 24° Réaumur (86° Fahrenheit) in the shade. Through the window one could see kerchiefed peasant girls weeding a garden path on their hands and knees or gently raking the sun-mottled sand. (The happy days when they would be cleaning streets and digging canals for the State were still beyond the horizon.) Golden orioles in the greenery emitted their four brilliant notes: dee-del-dee-O!

Ned lumbered past the window in a fair impersonation of the gardener's mate Ivan (who was to become in 1918 a member of the local Soviet). On later pages longer words appeared; and at the very end of the brown, inkstained volume, a real, sensible story unfolded its adult sentences ('One day Ted said to Ann: Let us – '), the little reader's ultimate triumph and reward. I was thrilled by the thought that some day I might attain such proficiency. The magic has endured, and whenever a grammar book comes my way, I instantly turn to the last page to enjoy a forbidden glimpse of the laborious student's future, of that promised land where, at last, words are meant to mean what they mean.

Summer *soomerki* – the lovely Russian word for dusk. Time: a dim point in the first decade of this unpopular century. Place: latitude 59° north from your equator, longitude 100° east from my writing hand. The day would take hours to fade, and everything – sky, tall flowers, still water – would be kept in a state of infinite vesperal suspense, deepened rather than resolved by the doleful moo of a cow in a distant meadow or by the still more moving cry that came from some bird beyond the lower course of the river, where the vast expanse of a misty-blue sphagnum bog, because of its mystery and remoteness, the Rukavishnikov children had baptized America.

In the drawing room of our country house, before going to bed, I would often be read to in English by my mother. As she came to a particularly dramatic passage, where the hero was about to encounter some strange, perhaps fatal danger, her voice would slow down, her words would be spaced portentously, and before turning the pages she would place upon it her hand, with its familiar pigeon-blood ruby and diamond ring (within the limpid facets of which, had I been a better crystal-gazer, I might have seen a room, people, lights, trees in the rain – a whole period of émigré life for which that ring was to pay).

There were tales about knights whose terrific but wonderfully aseptic wounds were bathed by damsels in grottoes. From a windswept clifftop, a medieval maiden with flying hair and a youth in hose gazed at the round Isles of the Blessed. In 'Misunderstood,' the fate of Humphrey used to bring a more specialized lump to one's throat than anything in Dickens or

Daudet (great devisers of lumps), while a shamelessly allegorical story, 'Beyond the Blue Mountains,' dealing with two pairs of little travelers – good Clover and Cowslip, bad Buttercup and Daisy – contained enough exciting details to make one forget its 'message.'

There were also those large, flat, glossy picture books. I particularly liked the blue-coated, red-trousered, coal-black Golliwogg, with underclothes buttons for eyes, and his meager harem of five wooden dolls. By the illegal method of cutting themselves frocks out of the American flag (Peg taking the motherly stripes, Sarah Jane the pretty stars) two of the dolls acquired a certain soft femininity, once their neutral articulations had been clothed. The Twins (Meg and Weg) and the Midget remained stark naked and, consequently, sexless.

We see them in the dead of night stealing out of doors to sling snowballs at one another until the chimes of a remote clock ('But Hark!' comments the rhymed text) send them back to their toybox in the nursery. A rude jack-in-the-box shoots out, frightening my lovely Sarah, and that picture I heartily disliked because it reminded me of children's parties at which this or that graceful little girl, who had bewitched me, happened to pinch her finger or hurt her knee, and would forthwith expand into a purple-faced goblin, all wrinkles and bawling mouth. Another time they went on a bicycle journey and were captured by cannibals; our unsuspecting travelers had been quenching their thirst at a palm-fringed pool when the tom-toms sounded. Over the shoulder of my past I admire again the crucial picture: the Golliwogg, still on his knees by the pool but no longer drinking; his hair stands on end and the normal black of his face has changed to a weird ashen hue. 23

There was also the motorcar book (Sarah Jane, always my favorite, sporting a long green veil), with the usual sequel – crutches and bandaged heads.

And, yes – the airship. Yards and yards of yellow silk went to make it, and an additional tiny balloon was provided for the sole use of the fortunate Midget. At the immense altitude to which the ship reached, the aeronauts huddled together for warmth while the lost little soloist, still the object of my intense envy notwithstanding his plight, drifted into an abyss of frost and stars – alone.

3

I next see my mother leading me bedward through the enormous hall, where a central flight of stairs swept up and up, with nothing but hothouse-like panes of glass between the upper landing and the light green evening sky. One would lag back and shuffle and slide a little on the smooth stone floor of the hall, causing the gentle hand at the small of one's back to propel one's reluctant frame by means of indulgent pushes. Upon reaching the stairway, my custom was to get to the steps by squirming under the handrail between the newel post and the first banister. With every new summer, the process of squeezing through became more difficult; nowadays, even my ghost would get stuck.

Another part of the ritual was to ascend with closed eyes. 'Step, step, step,' came my mother's voice as she led me up – and sure enough, the surface of the next tread would receive the blind child's confident foot; all one had to do was lift it a little higher than usual, so as to avoid stubbing one's toe against the riser. This slow, somewhat somnambulistic ascension in self-engendered darkness held obvious delights. The keenest of them was not knowing when the last step would come. At the top of the stairs, one's foot would be automatically lifted to the deceptive call of 'Step,' and then, with a momentary sense of exquisite panic, with a wild contraction of muscles, would sink into the phantasm of a step, padded, as it were, with the infinitely elastic stuff of its own nonexistence.

It is surprising what method there was in my bedtime dawdling. True, the whole going-up-the-stairs business now reveals certain transcendental values. Actually, however, I was merely playing for time by extending every second to its utmost. This would still go on when my mother turned me over, to be undressed, to Miss Clayton or Mademoiselle.

There were five bathrooms in our country house, and a medley of venerable washstands (one of these I would seek out in its dark nook whenever I had been crying, so as to feel on my swollen face which I was ashamed to show, the healing touch of its groping jet while I stepped on the rusty pedal). Regular baths were taken in the evening. For morning ablutions, the round, rubber English tubs were used. Mine was about four feet in diameter, with a knee-high rim. Upon the lathered back of the squatting child, a jugful of water was carefully poured by an aproned servant. Its temperature varied with the hydrotherapeutic notions of successive mentors. There was that bleak period of dawning puberty, when an icy deluge was decreed by our current tutor, who happened to be a medical student. On the other hand, the temperature of one's evening bath remained pleasantly constant at 28° Réaumur (95°

Fahrenheit) as measured by a large kindly thermometer whose wooden sheathing (with a bit of damp string in the eye of the handle) allowed it to share in the buoyancy of celluloid gold-fishes and little swans.

The toilets were separate from the bathrooms, and the oldest among them was a rather sumptuous but gloomy affair with some fine panelwork and a tasseled rope of red velvet, which, when pulled, produced a beautifully modulated, discreetly muffled gurgle and gulp. From that corner of the house, one could see Hesperus and hear the nightingales, and it was there that, later, I used to compose my youthful verse, dedicated to unembraced beauties, and morosely survey, in a dimly illumin-ated mirror, the immediate erection of a strange castle in an unknown Spain. As a small child, however, I was assigned a more modest arrangement, rather casually situated in a narrow recess between a wicker hamper and the door leading to the nursery bathroom. This door I liked to keep ajar; through it I drowsily looked at the shimmer of steam above the mahogany bath, at the fantastic flotilla of swans and skiffs, at myself with a harp in one of the boats, at a furry moth pinging against the reflector of the kerosene lamp, at the stained-glass window beyond, at its two halberdiers consisting of colored rectangles. Bending from my warm seat, I liked to press the middle of my brow, its ophryon to be precise, against the smooth comfortable edge of the door and then roll my head a little, so that the door would move to and fro while its edge remained all the time in soothing contact with my forehead. A dreamy rhythm would permeate my being. The recent 'Step, step, step,' would be taken up by a dripping faucet. And, fruitfully combining rhythmic pattern with rhythmic sound, I would unravel the labyrinthian frets on the linoleum, and find faces where a crack or a shadow afforded a *point de repère* for the eye. I appeal to parents: never, never say, 'Hurry up,' to a child.

The final stage in the course of my vague navigation would come when I reached the island of my bed. From the veranda or drawing room, where life was going on without me, my mother would come up for the warm murmur of her good-night kiss. Closed inside shutters, a lighted candle, Gentle Jesus, meek and mild, something-something little child, the child kneeling on the pillow that presently would engulf his humming head. English prayers and the little icon featuring a sun-tanned Greek Catholic saint formed an innocent association upon which I look back with pleasure; and above the icon, high up on the wall, where the shadow of something (of the bamboo screen between bed and door?) undulated in the warm candle-light, a framed aquarelle showed a dusky path winding through one of those eerily dense European beechwoods, where the only undergrowth is bindweed and the only sound one's thumping heart. In an English fairy tale my mother had once read to me, a small boy stepped out of his bed into a picture and rode his hobbyhorse along a painted path between silent trees. While I knelt on my pillow in a mist of drowsiness and talc-powdered well-being, half sitting on my calves and rapidly going through my prayer, I imagined the motion of climbing into the picture above my bed and plunging into that enchanted beechwood – which I did visit in due time.

A bewildering sequence of English nurses and governesses, some of them wringing their hands, others smiling at me enigmatically, come out to meet me as I re-enter my past.

There was dim Miss Rachel, whom I remember mainly in terms of Huntley and Palmer biscuits (the nice almond rocks at the top of the blue-papered tin box, the insipid cracknels at the bottom) which she unlawfully shared with me after my teeth had been brushed. There was Miss Clayton, who, when I slumped in my chair, would poke me in the middle vertebrae and then smilingly throw back her own shoulders to show what she wanted of me: she told me a nephew of hers at my age (four) used to breed caterpillars, but those she collected for me in an open jar with nettles all walked away one morning, and the gardener said they had hanged themselves. There was lovely, black-haired, aquamarine-eyed Miss Norcott, who lost a white kid glove at Nice or Beaulieu, where I vainly looked for it on the shingly beach among the colored pebbles and the glaucous lumps of sea-changed bottle glass. Lovely Miss Norcott was asked to leave at once, one night at Abbazia. She embraced me in the morning twilight of the nursery, pale-mackintoshed and weeping like a Babylonian willow, and that day I remained inconsolable, despite the hot chocolate that the Petersons' old Nanny had made especially for me and the special bread and butter, on the smooth surface of which my aunt Nata, adroitly capturing my attention, drew a daisy, then a cat, and then the little mermaid whom I had just been reading about with Miss Norcott and crying over, too, so I started to cry again. There was myopic little Miss Hunt, whose short stay with us in

Wiesbaden came to an end the day my brother and I – aged four and five, respectively – managed to evade her nervous vigilance by boarding a steamer that took us quite a way down the Rhine before recapture. There was pink-nosed Miss Robinson. There was Miss Clayton again. There was one awful person who read to me Marie Corelli's *The Mighty Atom*. There were still others. At a certain point they faded out of my life. French and Russian took over; and what little time remained for the speaking of English was devoted to occasional sessions with two gentlemen, Mr Burness and Mr Cummings, neither of whom dwelt with us. They are associated in my mind with winters in St Petersburg, where we had a house on the Morskaya Street.

Mr Burness was a large Scotsman with a florid face, light-blue eyes and lank, straw-colored hair. He spent his mornings teaching at a language school and then crammed into the afternoon more private lessons than the day could well hold. Traveling, as he did, from one part of the town to another and having to depend on the torpid trot of dejected *izvozchik* (cab) horses to get him to his pupils, he would be, with luck, only a quarter of an hour late for his two o'clock lesson (wherever that was), but would arrive after five for his four o'clock one. The tension of waiting for him and hoping that, for once, his superhuman doggedness might balk before the gray wall of some special snowstorm was the kind of feeling that one trusts never to meet with in mature life (but that I did experience again when circumstances forced me, in my turn, to give lessons and when, in my furnished rooms in Berlin, I awaited a certain stone-faced pupil, who would *always* turn up despite the obstacles I mentally piled in his way).

The very darkness that was gathering outside seemed a waste product of Mr Burness' efforts to reach our house. Presently the valet would come to drop the blue voluminous blinds and draw the flowered window draperies. The tick-tock of the grandfather's clock in the schoolroom gradually assumed a dreary, nagging intonation. The tightness of my shorts in the groin and the rough touch of ribbed black stockings rubbing against the tender inside of my bent legs would mingle with the dull pressure of a humble need, the satisfaction of which I kept postponing. Nearly an hour would pass and there would be no sign of Mr Burness. My brother would go to his room and play some practice piece on the piano and then plunge and replunge into some of the melodies that I loathed – the instruction to the artificial flowers in *Faust* (. . . *dites-lui qu'elle est belle* . . .) or Vladimir Lenski's wail (. . . *Koo-dah, koo-dah, koo-dah vï udalilis*'). I would leave the upper floor, where we children dwelt, and slowly slide along the balustrade down to the second story, where my parents' rooms were situated. As often as not, they used to be out at that time, and in the gathering dusk the place acted upon my young senses in a curiously teleological way, as if this accumulation of familiar things in the dark were doing its utmost to form the definite and permanent image that repeated exposure did finally leave in my mind.

The sepia gloom of an arctic afternoon in midwinter invaded the rooms and was deepening to an oppressive black. A bronze angle, a surface of glass or polished mahogany here and there in the darkness, reflected the odds and ends of light from the street, where the globes of tall street lamps along its middle line were already diffusing their lunar glow. Gauzy shadows moved on the ceiling. In the stillness, the dry sound of a chrysanthemum petal falling upon the marble of a table made one's nerves twang.

My mother's boudoir had a convenient oriel for looking out on the Morskaya in the direction of the Maria Square. With lips pressed against the thin fabric that veiled the windowpane I would gradually taste the cold of the glass through the gauze. From that oriel, some years later, at the outbreak of the Revolution, I watched various engagements and saw my first dead man: he was being carried away on a stretcher, and from one dangling leg an ill-shod comrade kept trying to pull off the boot despite pushes and punches from the stretchermen – all this at a goodish trot. But in the days of Mr Burness' lessons there was nothing to watch save the dark, muffled street and its receding line of loftily suspended lamps, around which the snowflakes passed and repassed with a graceful, almost deliberately slackened motion, as if to show how the trick was done and how simple it was. From another angle, one might see a more generous stream of snow in a brighter, violet-tinged nimbus of gaslight, and then the jutting enclosure where I stood would seem to drift slowly up and up, like a balloon. At last one of the phantom sleighs gliding along the street would come to a stop, and with gawky haste Mr Burness in his fox-furred *shapka* would make for our door.

From the schoolroom, whither I had preceded him, I would hear his vigorous footsteps crashing nearer and nearer, and, no matter how cold the day was, his good, ruddy face would be sweating abundantly as he strode in. I remember the terrific energy with which he pressed on the spluttering pen as he wrote down, in the roundest of round hands, the tasks to be   31 prepared for the next day. Usually at the end of the lesson a certain limerick was asked for and granted, the point of the performance being that the word 'screamed' in it was to be involuntarily enacted by oneself every time Mr Burness gave a formidable squeeze to the hand he held in his beefy paw as he recited the lines:

> There was a young lady from Russia
> Who (squeeze) whenever you'd crush her.
> She (squeeze) and she (squeeze) . . .

by which time the pain would have become so excruciating that we never got any farther.

5

The quiet, bearded gentleman with a stoop, old-fashioned Mr Cummings, who taught me, in 1907 or 1908, to draw, had been my mother's drawing master also. He had come to Russia in the early nineties as foreign correspondent and illustrator for the London *Graphic*. Marital misfortunes were rumored to obscure his life. A melancholy sweetness of manner made up for the meagerness of his talent. He wore an ulster unless the weather was very mild, when he would switch to the kind of greenish-brown woolen cloak called a *loden*.

I was captivated by his use of the special eraser he kept in his waistcoat pocket, by the manner in which he held the page taut, and afterwards flicked off, with the back of his fingers, the 'gutticles of the percha' (as he said). Silently, sadly, he illustrated for me the marble laws of perspective: long, straight

strokes of his elegantly held, incredibly sharp pencil caused the
lines of the room he created out of nothing (abstract walls,
receding ceiling and floor) to come together in one remote
hypothetical point with tantalizing and sterile accuracy.
Tantalizing, because it made me think of railway tracks, sym-
metrically and trickily converging before the bloodshot eyes of
my favorite mask, a grimy engine driver; sterile, because that
room remained unfurnished and quite empty, being devoid
even of the neutral statues one finds in the uninteresting first
hall of a museum.

The rest of the picture gallery made up for its gaunt vestibule. Mr Cummings was a master of the sunset. His little
watercolors, purchased at different times for five or ten roubles
apiece by members of our household, led a somewhat precarious existence, shifting, as they did, to more and more obscure
nooks and finally getting completely eclipsed by some sleek
porcelain beast or a newly framed photograph. After I had
learned not only to draw cubes and cones but to shade properly
with smooth, merging slants such parts of them as had to be
made to turn away forever, the kind old gentleman contented
himself with painting under my enchanted gaze his own wet
little paradises, variations of one landscape: a summer evening
with an orange sky, a pasture ending in the black fringe of a
distant forest, and a luminous river, repeating the sky and
winding away and away.

Later on, from around 1910 to 1912, the well-known
'impressionist' (a term of the period) Yaremich took over; a
humorless and formless person, he advocated a 'bold' style,
blotches of dull color, smears of sepia and olive-brown, by
means of which I had to reproduce on huge sheets of gray

paper, humanoid shapes that we modeled of plasticine and placed in 'dramatic' positions against a backcloth of velvet with all kinds of folds and shadow effects. It was a depressing combination of at least three different arts, all approximate, and finally I rebelled.

He was replaced by the celebrated Dobuzhinski who liked to give me his lessons on the *piano nobile* of our house, in one of its pretty reception rooms downstairs, which he entered in a particularly noiseless way as if afraid to startle me from my verse-making stupor. He made me depict from memory, in the greatest possible detail, objects I had certainly seen thousands of times without visualizing them properly: a street lamp, a postbox, the tulip design on the stained glass of our own front door. He tried to teach me to find the geometrical coordinations between the slender twigs of a leafless boulevard tree, a system of visual give-and-takes, requiring a precision of linear expression, which I failed to achieve in my youth, but applied gratefully, in my adult instar, not only to the drawing of butterfly genitalia during my seven years at the Harvard Museum of Comparative Zoology, when immersing myself in the bright wellhole of a microscope to record in India ink this or that new structure; but also, perhaps, to certain camera-lucida needs of literary composition. Emotionally, however, I am still more indebted to the earlier color treats given me by my mother and her former teacher. How readily Mr Cummings would sit down on a stool, part behind with both hands his – what? was he wearing a frock coat? I see only the gesture – and proceed to open the black tin paintbox. I loved the nimble way he had of soaking his paintbrush in multiple color to the accompaniment the rich reds and yellows that the brush dimpled were appetizingly cupped; and having thus collected its honey, it would cease to hover and poke, and, by two or three sweeps of its lush tip, would drench the 'Vatmanski' paper with an even spread of orange sky, across which, while that sky was still dampish, a long purple-black cloud would be laid. 'And that's all, dearie,' he would say. 'That's all there is to it.'

On one occasion, I had him draw an express train for me. I watched his pencil ably evolve the cowcatcher and elaborate headlights of a locomotive that looked as if it had been acquired secondhand for the Trans-Siberian line after it had done duty at Promontory Point, Utah, in the sixties. Then came five disappointingly plain carriages. When he had quite finished them, he carefully shaded the ample smoke coming from the huge funnel, cocked his head, and, after a moment of pleased contemplation, handed me the drawing. I tried to look pleased, too. He had forgotten the tender.

A quarter of a century later, I learned two things: that Burness, by then dead, had been well known in Edinburgh as a scholarly translator of the Russian romantic poems that had been the altar and frenzy of my boyhood; and that my humble drawing master, whose age I used to synchronize with that of granduncles and old family servants, had married a young Estonian girl about the time I myself married. When I learned these later developments, I experienced a queer shock; it was as if life had impinged upon my creative rights by wriggling on beyond the subjective limits so elegantly and economically set by childhood memories that I thought I had signed and sealed.

'And what about Yaremich?' I asked M. V. Dobuzhinski, 35

one summer afternoon in the nineteen-forties, as we strolled through a beech forest in Vermont. 'Is he remembered?'

'Indeed, he is,' replied Mstislav Valerianovich. 'He was exceptionally gifted. I don't know what kind of teacher he was, but I do know that *you* were the most hopeless pupil I ever had.'

O n a summer morning, in the legendary Russia of my boyhood, my first glance upon awakening was for the chink
between the white inner shutters. If it disclosed a watery pallor,
one had better not open them at all, and so be spared the sight
of a sullen day sitting for its picture in a puddle. How resent-
fully one would deduce, from a line of dull light, the leaden
sky, the sodden sand, the gruel-like mess of broken brown
blossoms under the lilacs – and that flat, fallow leaf (the first
casualty of the season) pasted upon a wet garden bench!

But if the chink was a long glint of dewy brilliancy, then I
made haste to have the window yield its treasure. With one
blow, the room would be cleft into light and shade. The foliage
of birches moving in the sun had the translucent green tone of
grapes, and in contrast to this there was the dark velvet of fir
trees against a blue of extraordinary intensity, the like of which
I rediscovered only many years later, in the montane zone of
Colorado.

From the age of seven, everything I felt in connexion with
a rectangle of framed sunlight was dominated by a single pas-
sion. If my first glance of the morning was for the sun, my first
thought was for the butterflies it would engender. The original
event had been banal enough. On the honeysuckle, overhanging
the carved back of a bench just opposite the main entrance,
my guiding angel (whose wings, except for the absence of a
Florentine limbus, resemble those of Fra Angelico's Gabriel) 37

pointed out to me a rare visitor, a splendid, pale-yellow creature with black blotches, blue crenels, and a cinnabar eyespot above each chrome-rimmed black tail. As it probed the inclined flower from which it hung, its powdery body slightly bent, it kept restlessly jerking its great wings, and my desire for it was one of the most intense I have ever experienced. Agile Ustin, our town-house janitor, who for a comic reason (explained elsewhere) happened to be that summer in the country with us, somehow managed to catch it in my cap, after which it was transferred, cap and all, to a wardrobe, where domestic naphthalene was fondly expected by Mademoiselle to kill it overnight. On the following morning, however, when she unlocked the wardrobe to take something out, my Swallowtail, with a mighty rustle, flew into her face, then made for the open window, and presently was but a golden fleck dipping and dodging and soaring eastward, over timber and tundra, to Vologda, Viatka and Perm, and beyond the gaunt Ural range to Yakutsk and Verkhne Kolymsk, and from Verkhne Kolymsk, where it lost a tail, to the fair Island of St Lawrence, and across Alaska to Dawson, and southward along the Rocky Mountains – to be finally overtaken and captured, after a forty-year race, on an immigrant dandelion under an endemic aspen near Boulder. In a letter from Mr Brune to Mr Rawlins, 14 June 1735, in the Bodleian collection, he states that one Mr Vernon followed a butterfly nine miles before he could catch him (*The Recreative Review or Eccentricities of Literature and Life*, Vol. 1, p. 144, London, 1821).

Soon after the wardrobe affair I found a spectacular moth, marooned in a corner of a vestibule window, and my mother dispatched it with ether. In later years, I used many killing agents, but the least contact with the initial stuff would always cause the porch of the past to light up and attract that blundering beauty. Once, as a grown man, I was under ether during appendectomy, and with the vividness of a decalcomania picture I saw my own self in a sailor suit mounting a freshly emerged Emperor moth under the guidance of a Chinese lady who I knew was my mother. It was all there, brilliantly reproduced in my dream, while my own vitals were being exposed: the soaking, ice-cold absorbent cotton pressed to the insect's lemurian head; the subsiding spasms of its body; the satisfying crackle produced by the pin penetrating the hard crust of its thorax; the careful insertion of the point of the pin in the cork-bottomed groove of the spreading board; the symmetrical adjustment of the thick, strong-veined wings under neatly affixed strips of semitransparent paper.

2

I must have been eight when, in a storeroom of our country house, among all kinds of dusty objects, I discovered some wonderful books acquired in the days when my mother's mother had been interested in natural science and had had a famous university professor of zoology (Shimkevich) give private lessons to her daughter. Some of these books were mere curios, such as the four huge brown folios of Albertus Seba's work (*Locupletissimi Rerum Naturalium Thesauri Accurata Descriptio* . . .), printed in Amsterdam around 1750. On their coarse-grained pages I found woodcuts of serpents and butterflies and embryos. The fetus of an Ethiopian female child hanging by the neck in a glass jar used to give me a nasty shock every time I came across it; nor did I much care for the stuffed hydra on plate CII, with its seven lion-toothed turtleheads on seven serpentine necks and its strange, bloated body which bore buttonlike tubercules along the sides and ended in a knotted tail.

Other books I found in that attic, among herbariums full of alpine columbines, and blue palemoniums, and Jove's campions, and orange-red lilies, and other Davos flowers, came closer to my subject. I took in my arms and carried downstairs glorious loads of fantastically attractive volumes: Maria Sibylla Merian's (1647–1717) lovely plates of Surinam insects, and Esper's noble *Die Schmetterlinge* (Erlangen, 1777), and Boisduval's *Icones Historiques de Lépidoptères Nouveaux ou Peu Connus* (Paris, begun in 1832). Still more exciting were the products of the latter half of the century – Newman's *Natural History of British Butterflies and Moths*, Hofmann's *Die Gross-Schmetterlinge Europas*, the Grand Duke Nikolay Mihailovich's *Mémoires* on Asiatic lepidoptera (with incomparably beautiful figures painted by Kavrigin, Rybakov, Lang), Scudder's stupendous work on the *Butterflies of New England*.

Retrospectively, the summer of 1905, though quite vivid in many ways, is not animated yet by a single bit of quick flutter or colored fluff around or across the walks with the village schoolmaster: the Swallowtail of June 1906 was still in the larval stage on a roadside umbellifer; but in the course of that month I became acquainted with a score or so of common things, and Mademoiselle was already referring to a certain forest road that culminated in a marshy meadow full of Small Pearl-bordered Fritillaries (thus called in my first unforgettable and unfadingly magical little manual, Richard South's *The Butterflies of the British Isles*, which had just come out at that time) as *le chemin des papillons bruns*. The following year I became aware that many of our butterflies and moths did not occur in England or Central Europe, and more complete atlases helped me to determine them. A severe illness (pneumonia, with fever up to 41° centigrade), in the beginning of 1907, mysteriously abolished the rather monstrous gift of numbers that had made of me a child prodigy during a few months (today I cannot multiply 13 by 17 without pencil and paper; I can add them up, though, in a trice, the teeth of the three fitting in neatly); but the butterflies survived. My mother accumulated a library and a museum around my bed, and the longing to describe a new species completely replaced that of discovering a new prime number. A trip to Biarritz, in August 1907, added new wonders (though not as lucid and numerous as they were to be in 1909). By 1908, I had gained absolute control over the European lepidoptera as known to Hofmann. By 1910, I had dreamed my way through the first volumes of Seitz's prodigious picture book *Die Gross-Schmetterlinge der Erde*, had purchased a number of rarities recently described, and was voraciously reading entomological periodicals, especially English and Russian ones. Great upheavals were taking place in the development of systematics. Since the middle of the century, Continental lepidopterology had been, on the whole, a simple and stable affair, smoothly run by the Germans. Its high priest, Dr Staudinger, was also the head of the largest firm of insect dealers. Even now, half a century after his death, German lepidopterists have not quite managed to shake off the hypnotic spell occasioned by his authority. He was still alive when his school began to lose ground as a scientific force in the world. While he and his followers stuck to specific and generic names sanctioned by long usage and were content to classify butterflies by characters visible to the naked eye, English-speaking authors were introducing nomenclatorial changes as a result of a strict application of the law of priority and taxonomic changes based on the microscopic study of organs. The Germans did their best to ignore the new trends and continued to cherish the philately-like side of entomology. Their solicitude for the 'average collector who should not be made to dissect' is comparable to the way nervous publishers of popular novels pamper the 'average reader' – who should not be made to think.

There was another more general change, which coincided with my ardent adolescent interest in butterflies and moths. The Victorian and Staudingerian kind of species, hermetic and homogeneous, with sundry (alpine, polar, insular, etc.) 'varieties' affixed to it from the outside, as it were, like incidental appendages, was replaced by a new, multiform and fluid kind of species, organically *consisting* of geographical races or subspecies. The evolutionary aspects of the case were thus brought out more clearly, by means of more flexible methods of classification, and further links between butterflies and the central problems of nature were provided by biological investigations.

The mysteries of mimicry had a special attraction for me. Its phenomena showed an artistic perfection usually associated with man-wrought things. Consider the imitation of oozing poison by bubblelike macules on a wing (complete with pseudo-refraction) or by glossy yellow knobs on a chrysalis ('Don't eat me – I have already been squashed, sampled and rejected').

Consider the tricks of an acrobatic caterpillar (of the Lobster Moth) which in infancy looks like bird's dung, but after molting develops scrabbly hymenopteroid appendages and baroque characteristics, allowing the extraordinary fellow to play two parts at once (like the actor in Oriental shows who *becomes* a pair of intertwisted wrestlers): that of a writhing larva and that of a big ant seemingly harrowing it. When a certain moth resembles a certain wasp in shape and color, it also walks and moves its antennae in a waspish, unmothlike manner. When a butterfly has to look like a leaf, not only are all the details of a leaf beautifully rendered but markings mimicking grub-bored holes are generously thrown in. 'Natural selection,' in the Darwinian sense, could not explain the miraculous coincidence of imitative aspect and imitative behavior, nor could one appeal to the theory of 'the struggle for life' when a protective device was carried to a point of mimetic subtlety, exuberance, and luxury far in excess of a predator's power of appreciation. I discovered in nature the nonutilitarian delights that I sought in art. Both were a form of magic, both were a game of intricate enchantment and deception.

3

I have hunted butterflies in various climes and disguises: as a pretty boy in knickerbockers and sailor cap; as a lanky cosmopolitan expatriate in flannel bags and beret; as a fat hatless old man in shorts. Most of my cabinets have shared the fate of our Vyra house. Those in our town house and the small addendum I left in the Yalta Museum have been destroyed, no doubt, by carpet beetles and other pests. A collection of South European stuff that I started in exile vanished in Paris during World War Two. All my American captures from 1940 to 1960 (several thousands of specimens including great rarities and types) are in the Mus. of Comp. Zoology, the Am. Nat. Hist. Mus., and the Cornell Univ. Mus. of Entomology, where they are safer than they would be in Tomsk or Atomsk. Incredibly happy memories, quite comparable, in fact, to those of my Russian boyhood, are associated with my research work at the MCZ, Cambridge, Mass. (1941–8). No less happy have been the many collecting trips taken almost every summer, during twenty years, through most of the states of my adopted country.

In Jackson Hole and in the Grand Canyon, on the mountain slopes above Telluride, Colo., and on a celebrated pine barren near Albany, N.Y., dwell, and will dwell, in generations more numerous than editions, the butterflies I have described as new. Several of my finds have been dealt with by other workers; some have been named after me. One of these, Nabokov's Pug (*Eupithecia nabokovi* McDunnough), which I boxed one night in 1943 on a picture window of James Laughlin's Alta Lodge in Utah, fits most philosophically into the thematic spiral that began in a wood on the Oredezh around 1910 – or perhaps even earlier, on that Nova Zemblan river a century and a half ago.

Few things indeed have I known in the way of emotion or appetite, ambition or achievement, that could surpass in richness and strength the excitement of entomological exploration. From the very first it had a great many interwinkling facets. One of them was the acute desire to be alone, since any companion, no matter how quiet, interfered with the concentrated enjoyment of my mania. Its gratification admitted of no compromise or exception. Already when I was ten, tutors and governesses knew that the morning was mine and cautiously kept away.

In this connexion, I remember the visit of a schoolmate, a boy of whom I was very fond and with whom I had excellent fun. He arrived one summer night – in 1913, I think – from a town some twenty-five miles away. His father had recently perished in an accident, the family was ruined and the stout-hearted lad, not being able to afford the price of a railway ticket, had bicycled all those miles to spend a few days with me.

On the morning following his arrival, I did everything I could to get out of the house for my morning hike without his knowing where I had gone. Breakfastless, with hysterical haste, I gathered my net, pill boxes, killing jar, and escaped through the window. Once in the forest, I was safe; but still I walked on, my calves quaking, my eyes full of scalding tears, the whole of me twitching with shame and self-disgust, as I visualized my poor friend, with his long pale face and black tie, moping in the hot garden – patting the panting dogs for want of something better to do, and trying hard to justify my absence to himself.

Let me look at my demon objectively. With the exception of my parents, no one really understood my obsession, and it was many years before I met a fellow sufferer. One of the first things I learned was not to depend on others for the growth of my collection. One summer afternoon, in 1911, Mademoiselle came into my room, book in hand, started to say she wanted to show me how wittily Rousseau denounced zoology (in favour of botany), and by then was too far gone in the gravitational process of lowering her bulk into an armchair to be stopped by my howl of anguish: on that seat I had happened to leave a glass-lidded cabinet tray with long, lovely series of the Large White. Her first reaction was one of stung vanity: her weight, surely, could not be accused of damaging what in fact it had demolished; her second was to console me: *Allons donc, ce ne sont que des papillons de potager!* – which only made matters worse. A Sicilian pair recently purchased from Staudinger had been crushed and bruised. A huge Biarritz example was utterly mangled. Smashed, too, were some of my choicest local captures. Of these, an aberration resembling the Canarian race of the species might have been mended with a few drops of glue; but a precious gynandromorph, left side male, right side female, whose abdomen could not be traced and whose wings had come off, was lost forever: one might reattach the wings but one could not prove that all four belonged to that headless thorax on its bent pin. Next morning, with an air of great mystery, poor Mademoiselle set off for St Petersburg and came back in the evening bringing me ('something better than your cabbage butterflies') a banal Urania moth mounted on plaster. 'How you hugged me, how you danced with joy!' she exclaimed ten years later in the course of inventing a brand-new past.

Our country doctor, with whom I had left the pupae of a rare moth when I went on a journey abroad, wrote me that everything had hatched finely; but in reality a mouse had got at the precious pupae, and upon my return the deceitful old man produced some common Tortoiseshell butterflies, which, I presume, he had hurriedly caught in his garden and popped into the breeding cage as plausible substitutes (so *he* thought).

Better than he, was an enthusiastic kitchen boy who would

sometimes borrow my equipment and come back two hours later in triumph with a bagful of seething invertebrate life and several additional items. Loosening the mouth of the net which he had tied up with a string, he would pour out his cornucopian spoil – a mass of grasshoppers, some sand, the two parts of a mushroom he had thriftily plucked on the way home, more grasshoppers, more sand, and one battered Small White.

In the works of major Russian poets I can discover only two lepidopteral images of genuinely sensuous quality: Bunin's impeccable evocation of what is certainly a Tortoiseshell:

> And there will fly into the room
> A colored butterfly in silk
> To flutter, rustle and pit-pat
> On the blue ceiling . . .

and Fet's 'Butterfly' soliloquizing:

> Whence have I come and whither am I hasting
> Do not inquire;
> Now on a graceful flower I have settled
> And now respire.

In French poetry one is struck by Musset's well-known lines (in *Le Saule*):

> *Le phalène doré dans sa course légère*
> *Traverse les prés embaumés*

which is an absolutely exact description of the crepuscular flight of the male of the geometrid called in England the Orange moth; and there is Fargue's fascinatingly apt phrase (in *Les Quatres Journées*) about a garden which, at nightfall, *se glace de bleu comme l'aile du grand Sylvain* (the Poplar Admirable). 47

And among the very few genuine lepidopterological images in
English poetry, my favorite is Browning's

> On our other side is the straight-up rock;
> And a path is kept 'twixt the gorge and it
> By boulder-stones where lichens mock
> The marks on a moth, and small ferns fit
> Their teeth to the polished block.
>
> *('By the Fire-side')*

It is astounding how little the ordinary person notices butterflies. 'None,' calmly replied that sturdy Swiss hiker with Camus
in his rucksack when purposely asked by me for the benefit of
my incredulous companion if he had seen any butterflies while
descending the trail where, a moment before, you and I had
been delighting in swarms of them. It is also true that when I
call up the image of a particular path remembered in minute
detail but pertaining to a summer before that of 1906, preced-
ing, that is, the date of my first locality label, and never
revisited, I fail to make out one wing, one wingbeat, one azure
flash, one moth-gemmed flower, as if an evil spell had been
cast on the Adriatic coast making all its 'leps' (as the slangier
among us say) invisible. Exactly thus an entomologist may
feel some day when plodding beside a jubilant, and already
helmetless botanist amid the hideous flora of a parallel planet,
with not a single insect in sight; and thus (in odd proof of the
odd fact that whenever possible the scenery of our infancy is
used by an economically minded producer as a ready-made
setting for our adult dreams) the seaside hilltop of a certain
recurrent nightmare of mine, whereinto I smuggle a collapsible
48   net from my waking state, is gay with thyme and melilot, but

incomprehensibly devoid of all the butterflies that should be there.

I also found out very soon that a 'lepist' indulging in his quiet quest was apt to provoke strange reactions in other creatures. How often, when a picnic had been arranged, and I would be self-consciously trying to get my humble implements unnoticed into the tar-smelling charabanc (a tar preparation was used to keep flies away from the horses) or the tea-smelling Opel convertible (benzine forty years ago smelled that way), some cousin or aunt of mine would remark: 'Must you *really* take that net with you? Can't you enjoy yourself like a normal boy? Don't you think you are spoiling everybody's pleasure?' Near a sign NACH BODENLAUBE, at Bad Kissingen, Bavaria, just as I was about to join for a long walk my father and majestic old Muromtsev (who, four years before, in 1906, had been President of the first Russian Parliament), the latter turned his marble head toward me, a vulnerable boy of eleven, and said with his famous solemnity: 'Come with us by all means, but do not chase butterflies, child. It spoils the rhythm of the walk.' On a path above the Black Sea, in the Crimea, among shrubs in waxy bloom, in March 1918, a bow-legged Bolshevik sentry attempted to arrest me for signaling (with my net, he said) to a British warship. In the summer of 1929, every time I walked through a village in the Eastern Pyrenees, and happened to look back, I would see in my wake the villagers frozen in the various attitudes my passage had caught them in, as if I were Sodom and they Lot's wife. A decade later, in the Maritime Alps, I once noticed the grass undulate in a serpentine way behind me because a fat rural policeman was wriggling after me on his belly to find out if I were not trapping songbirds. 49

America has shown even more of this morbid interest in my retiary activities than other countries have – perhaps because I was in my forties when I came there to live, and the older the man, the queerer he looks with a butterfly net in his hand. Stern farmers have drawn my attention to NO FISHING signs; from cars passing me on the highway have come wild howls of derision; sleepy dogs, though unmindful of the worst bum, have perked up and come at me, snarling; tiny tots have pointed me out to their puzzled mamas; broad-minded vacationists have asked me whether I was catching bugs for bait; and one morning on a wasteland, lit by tall yuccas in bloom, near Santa Fe, a big black mare followed me for more than a mile.

4

When, having shaken off all pursuers, I took the rough, red road that ran from our Vyra house toward field and forest, the animation and luster of the day seemed like a tremor of sympathy around me.

Very fresh, very dark Arran Browns, which emerged only every second year (conveniently, retrospection has fallen here into line), flitted among the firs or revealed their red markings and checkered fringes as they sunned themselves on the roadside bracken. Hopping above the grass, a diminutive Ringlet called Hero dodged my net. Several moths, too, were flying – gaudy sun lovers that sail from flower to flower like painted flies, or male insomniacs in search of hidden females, such as that rust-colored Oak Eggar hurtling across the shrubbery. I
50 noticed (one of the major mysteries of my childhood) a soft

pale green wing caught in a spider's web (by then I knew what it was: part of a Large Emerald). The tremendous larva of the Goat Moth, ostentatiously segmented, flat-headed, flesh-colored and glossily flushed, a strange creature 'as naked as a worm' to use a French comparison, crossed my path in frantic search for a place to pupate (the awful pressure of metamorphosis, the aura of a disgraceful fit in a public place). On the bark of that birch tree, the stout one near the park wicket, I had found last spring a dark aberration of Sievers' Carmelite (just another gray moth to the reader). In the ditch, under the bridgelet, a bright-yellow Silvius Skipper hobnobbed with a dragonfly (just a blue libellula to me). From a flower head two male Coppers rose to a tremendous height, fighting all the way up – and then, after a while, came the downward flash of one of them returning to his thistle. These were familiar insects, but at any moment something better might cause me to stop with a quick intake of breath. I remember one day when I warily brought my net closer and closer to an uncommon Hairstreak that had daintily settled on a sprig. I could clearly see the white W on its chocolate-brown underside. Its wings were closed and the inferior ones were rubbing against each other in a curious circular motion – possibly producing some small, blithe crepitation pitched too high for a human ear to catch. I had long wanted that particular species, and, when near enough, I struck. You have heard champion tennis players moan after muffing an easy shot. You may have seen the face of the world-famous grandmaster Wilhelm Edmundson when, during a simultaneous display in a Minsk café, he lost his rook, by an absurd oversight, to the local amateur and pediatrician, Dr Schach, who eventually won. But that day nobody (except my older self) could see me shake out a piece of twig from an otherwise empty net and stare at a hole in the tarlatan.

5

Near the intersection of two carriage roads (one, well-kept, running north-south in between our 'old' and 'new' parks, and the other, muddy and rutty, leading, if you turned west, to Batovo) at a spot where aspens crowded on both sides of a dip, I would be sure to find in the third week of June great blue-black nymphalids striped with pure white, gliding and wheeling low above the rich clay which matched the tint of their undersides when they settled and closed their wings. Those were the dung-loving males of what the old Aurelians used to call the Poplar Admirable, or, more exactly, they belonged to its Bucovinan subspecies. As a boy of nine, not knowing that race, I noticed how much our North Russian specimens differed from the Central European form figured in Hofmann, and rashly wrote to Kuznetsov, one of the greatest Russian, or indeed world, lepidopterists of all time, naming my new subspecies 'Limenitis populi rossica.' A long month later he returned my description and aquarelle of 'rossica Nabokov' with only two words scribbled on the back of my letter: 'bucovinensis Hormuzaki.' How I hated Hormuzaki! And how hurt I was when in one of Kuznetsov's later papers I found a gruff reference to 'schoolboys who keep naming minute varieties of the Poplar Nymph!' Undaunted, however, by the *populi* flop, I 'discovered' the following year a 'new' moth. That summer I had been collecting assiduously on moonless nights, in a glade of the park, by spreading a bedsheet over the grass and its annoyed glow-worms, and casting upon it the light of an acetylene lamp (which, six years later, was to shine on Tamara). Into that arena of radiance, moths would come drifting out of the solid blackness around me, and it was in that manner, upon that magic sheet, that I took a beautiful *Plusia* (now *Phytometra*) which, as I saw at once, differed from its closest ally by its mauve-and-maroon (instead of golden-brown) forewings, and narrower bractea mark and was not recognizably figured in any of my books. I sent its description and picture to Richard South, for publication in *The Entomologist*. He did not know it either, but with the utmost kindness checked it in the British Museum collection – and found it had been described long ago as *Plusia excelsa* by Kretschmar. I received the sad news, which was most sympathetically worded ('. . . should be congratulated for obtaining . . . very rare Volgan thing . . . admirable figure . . .') with the utmost stoicism; but years later, by a pretty fluke (I know I should not point out these plums to people), I got even with the first discoverer of *my* moth by giving his own name to a blind man in a novel.

Let me also evoke the hawkmoths, the jets of my boyhood! Colors would die a long death on June evenings. The lilac shrubs in full bloom before which I stood, net in hand, displayed clusters of a fluffy gray in the dusk – the ghost of purple. A moist young moon hung above the mist of a neighboring meadow. In many a garden have I stood thus in later years – in Athens, Antibes, Atlanta – but never have I waited with such a keen desire as before those darkening lilacs. And suddenly it would come, the low buzz passing from flower to flower, the vibrational halo around the streamlined body of an olive and

53

pink Hummingbird moth poised in the air above the corolla into which it had dipped its long tongue. Its handsome black larva (resembling a diminutive cobra when it puffed out its ocellated front segments) could be found on dank willow herb two months later. Thus every hour and season had its delights. And, finally, on cold, or even frosty, autumn nights, one could sugar for moths by painting tree trunks with a mixture of molasses, beer, and rum. Through the gusty blackness, one's lantern would illumine the stickily glistening furrows of the bark and two or three large moths upon it imbibing the sweets, their nervous wings half open butterfly fashion, the lower ones exhibiting their incredible crimson silk from beneath the lichen-gray primaries. '*Catocala adultera!*' I would triumphantly shriek in the direction of the lighted windows of the house as I stumbled home to show my captures to my father.

6

The 'English' park that separated our house from the hayfields was an extensive and elaborate affair with labyrinthine paths, Turgenevian benches, and imported oaks among the endemic firs and birches. The struggle that had gone on since my grandfather's time to keep the park from reverting to the wild state always fell short of complete success. No gardener could cope with the hillocks of frizzly black earth that the pink hands of moles kept heaping on the tidy sand of the main walk. Weeds and fungi, and ridgelike tree roots crossed and recrossed the sun-flecked trials. Bears had been eliminated in the eighties, but an occasional moose still visited the grounds. On a picturesque boulder, a little mountain ash and a still smaller aspen had climbed, holding hands, like two clumsy, shy children. Other, more elusive trespassers – lost picnickers or merry villagers – would drive our hoary gamekeeper Ivan crazy by scrawling ribald words on the benches and gates. The disintegrating process continues still, in a different sense, for when, nowadays, I attempt to follow in memory the winding paths from one given point to another, I notice with alarm that there are many gaps, due to oblivion or ignorance, akin to the terra-incognita blanks map makers of old used to call 'sleeping beauties.'

Beyond the park, there were fields, with a continuous shimmer of butterfly wings over a shimmer of flowers – daisies, bluebells, scabious, and others – which now rapidly pass by me in a kind of colored haze like those lovely, lush meadows, never to be explored, that one sees from the diner on a transcontinental journey. At the end of this grassy wonderland, the forest rose like a wall. There I roamed, scanning the tree trunks (the enchanted, the silent part of a tree) for certain tiny moths, called Pugs in England – delicate little creatures that cling in the daytime to speckled surfaces, with which their flat wings and turned-up abdomens blend. There, at the bottom of that sea of sunshot greenery, I slowly spun round the great boles. Nothing in the world would have seemed sweeter to me than to be able to add, by a stroke of luck, some remarkable new species to the long list of Pugs already named by others. And my pied imagination, ostensibly, and almost grotesquely, groveling to my desire (but all the time, in ghostly conspiracies behind the scenes, coolly planning the most distant events of my destiny), kept providing me with hallucinatory samples of small print: '. . . the only specimen so far known . . .' '. . . the   55 only specimen known of *Eupithecia petropolitanata* was taken by a Russian schoolboy . . .' '. . . by a young Russian collector . . .' '. . . by myself in the Government of St Petersburg, Tsarskoe Selo District, in 1910 . . . 1911 . . . 1912 . . . 1913 . . .' And then, thirty years later, that blessed black night in the Wasatch Range.

At first – when I was, say, eight or nine – I seldom roamed farther than the fields and woods between Vyra and Batovo. Later, when aiming at a particular spot half-a-dozen miles or more distant, I would use a bicycle to get there with my net strapped to the frame; but not many forest paths were passable on wheels; it was possible to ride there on horseback, of course, but, because of our ferocious Russian tabanids, one could not leave a horse haltered in a wood for any length of time: my spirited bay almost climbed up the tree it was tied to one day trying to elude them: big fellows with watered-silk eyes and tiger bodies, and gray little runts with an even more painful proboscis, but much more sluggish: to dispatch two or three of these dingy tipplers with one crush of the gloved hand as they glued themselves to the neck of my mount afforded me a wonderful empathic relief (which a dipterist might not appreciate). Anyway, on my butterfly hunts I always preferred hiking to any other form of locomotion (except, naturally, a flying seat gliding leisurely over the plant mats and rocks of an unexplored mountain, or hovering just above the flowery roof of a rain forest); for when you walk, especially in a region you have studied well, there is an exquisite pleasure in departing from one's itinerary to visit, here and there by the wayside, this glade, that glen, this or that combination of soil and flora – to
56   drop in, as it were, on a familiar butterfly in his particular

habitat, in order to see if he has emerged, and if so, how he is doing.

There came a July day – around 1910, I suppose – when I felt the urge to explore the vast marshland beyond the Oredezh. After skirting the river for three or four miles, I found a rickety footbridge. While crossing over, I could see the huts of a hamlet on my left, apple trees, rows of tawny pine logs lying on a green bank, and the bright patches made on the turf by the scattered clothes of peasant girls, who, stark naked in shallow water, romped and yelled, heeding me as little as if I were the discarnate carrier of my present reminiscences.

On the other side of the river, a dense crowd of small, bright blue male butterflies that had been tippling on the rich, trampled mud and cow dung through which I trudged rose all together into the spangled air and settled again as soon as I had passed.

After making my way through some pine groves and alder scrub I came to the bog. No sooner had my ear caught the hum of diptera around me, the guttural cry of a snipe overhead, the gulping sound of the morass under my foot, than I knew I would find here quite special arctic butterflies, whose pictures, or, still better, nonillustrated descriptions I had worshiped for several seasons. And the next moment I was among them. Over the small shrubs of bog bilberry with fruit of a dim, dreamy blue, over the brown eye of stagnant water, over moss and mire, over the flower spikes of the fragrant bog orchid (the *nochnaya fialka* of Russian poets), a dusky little Fritillary bearing the name of a Norse goddess passed in low, skimming flight. Pretty Cordigera, a gemlike moth, buzzed all over its uliginose food plant. I pursued rose-margined Sulphurs, gray-marbled Satyrs. Unmindful of the mosquitoes that furred my forearms, I stooped with a grunt of delight to snuff out the life of some silver-studded lepidopteron throbbing in the folds of my net. Through the smells of the bog, I caught the subtle perfume of butterfly wings on my fingers, a perfume which varies with the species – vanilla, or lemon, or musk, or a musty, sweetish odor difficult to define. Still unsated, I pressed forward. At last I saw I had come to the end of the marsh. The rising ground beyond was a paradise of lupines, columbines, and pentstemons. Mariposa lilies bloomed under Ponderosa pines. In the distance, fleeting cloud shadows dappled the dull green of slopes above timber line, and the gray and white of Longs Peak.

I confess I do not believe in time. I like to fold my magic carpet, after use, in such a way as to superimpose one part of the pattern upon another. Let visitors trip. And the highest enjoyment of timelessness – in a landscape selected at random – is when I stand among rare butterflies and their food plants. This is ecstasy, and behind the ecstasy is something else, which is hard to explain. It is like a momentary vacuum into which rushes all that I love. A sense of oneness with sun and stone. A thrill of gratitude to whom it may concern – to the contrapuntal genius of human fate or to tender ghosts humoring a lucky mortal.

PENGUIN 60s

ISABEL ALLENDE · *Voices in My Ear*
NICHOLSON BAKER · *Playing Trombone*
LINDSEY BAREHAM · *The Little Book of Big Soups*
KAREN BLIXEN · *From the Ngong Hills*
DIRK BOGARDE · *Coming of Age*
ANTHONY BURGESS · *Childhood*
ANGELA CARTER · *Lizzie Borden*
CARLOS CASTANEDA · *The Sorcerer's Ring of Power*
ELIZABETH DAVID · *Peperonata and Other Italian Dishes*
RICHARD DAWKINS · *The Pocket Watchmaker*
GERALD DURRELL · *The Pageant of Fireflies*
RICHARD ELLMANN · *The Trial of Oscar Wilde*
EPICURUS · *Letter on Happiness*
MARIANNE FAITHFULL · *Year One*
KEITH FLOYD · *Hot and Spicy Floyd*
ALEXANDER FRATER · *Where the Dawn Comes Up Like Thunder*
ESTHER FREUD · *Meeting Bilal*
JOHN KENNETH GALBRAITH · *The Culture of Contentment*
ROB GRANT AND DOUG NAYLOR · *Scenes from the Dwarf*
ROBERT GRAVES · *The Gods of Olympus*
JANE GRIGSON · *Puddings*
SOPHIE GRIGSON · *From Sophie's Table*
KATHARINE HEPBURN · *Little Me*
SUSAN HILL · *The Badness Within Him*
ALAN HOLLINGHURST · *Adventures Underground*
BARRY HUMPHRIES · *Less is More Please*
HOWARD JACOBSON · *Expulsion from Paradise*
P. D. JAMES · *The Girl Who Loved Graveyards*
STEPHEN KING · *Umney's Last Case*
LAO TZU · *Tao Te Ching*
DAVID LEAVITT · *Chips Is Here*

PENGUIN 60s

READ MORE IN PENGUIN

For complete information about books available from Penguin and how to order them, please write to us at the appropriate address below. Please note that for copyright reasons the selection of books varies from country to country.

IN THE UNITED KINGDOM: Please write to *Dept. EP, Penguin Books Ltd, Bath Road, Harmondsworth, Middlesex UB7 0DA.*

IN THE UNITED STATES: Please write to *Consumer Sales, Penguin USA, P.O. Box 999, Dept. 17109, Bergenfield, New Jersey 07621-0120.* VISA and MasterCard holders call 1-800-253-6476 to order Penguin titles.

IN CANADA: Please write to *Penguin Books Canada Ltd, 10 Alcorn Avenue, Suite 300, Toronto, Ontario M4V 3B2.*

IN AUSTRALIA: Please write to *Penguin Books Australia Ltd, P.O. Box 257, Ringwood, Victoria 3134.*

IN NEW ZEALAND: Please write to *Penguin Books (NZ) Ltd, Private Bag 102902, North Shore Mail Centre, Auckland 10.*

IN INDIA: Please write to *Penguin Books India Pvt Ltd, 706 Eros Apartments, 56 Nehru Place, New Delhi 110 019.*

IN THE NETHERLANDS: Please write to *Penguin Books Netherlands bv, Postbus 3507, NL-1001 AH Amsterdam.*

IN GERMANY: Please write to *Penguin Books Deutschland GmbH, Metzlerstrasse 26, 60594 Frankfurt am Main.*

IN SPAIN: Please write to *Penguin Books S. A., Bravo Murillo 19, 1º B, 28015 Madrid.*

IN ITALY: Please write to *Penguin Italia s.r.l., Via Felice Casati 20, I-20124 Milano.*

IN FRANCE: Please write to *Penguin France S. A., 17 rue Lejeune, F-31000 Toulouse.*

IN JAPAN: Please write to *Penguin Books Japan, Ishikiribashi Building, 2-5-4, Suido, Bunkyo-ku, Tokyo 112.*

IN GREECE: Please write to *Penguin Hellas Ltd, Dimocritou 3, GR-106 71 Athens.*

IN SOUTH AFRICA: Please write to *Longman Penguin Southern Africa (Pty) Ltd, Private Bag X08, Bertsham 2013.*